Faith —

what it is and what it leads to

Faith —

what it is and what it leads to

Charles Haddon Spurgeon

Christian Focus Publications

First Christian Focus edition 1987
Reprinted 1989, 1993

Published by
Christian Focus Publications,
Geanies House,
Fearn, Tain,
Ross-shire IV20 1TW
Scotland

ISBN 0 906731 55 0

Printed and bound in Great Britain by
Cox and Wyman Ltd, Reading

Contents

		Page
Chapter 1	*The Object of Faith; or, to what Faith looks*	1
Chapter 2	*The Reason of Faith; or why doth any man believe, and whence doth his faith come?*	8
Chapter 3	*The Ground of the Sinner's Faith; or, on what ground he dares to believe on the Lord Jesus Christ*	11
Chapter 4	*The Warrant of Faith; or why it dares to trust in Christ*	17
Chapter 5	*The Result of Faith; or, how it speeds when it comes to Christ*	23
Chapter 6	*The Satisfactory Declaration made in Scripture concerning those who have Faith*	28
Chapter 7	*Misapprehensions respecting it, by reason of which Christians are often cast down*...	37
Chapter 8	*What this Faith Includes*	44
Chapter 9	*What this Faith Excludes*	47

Foreword

The essential simple nature of the Christian faith as summed up by the apostle Paul, 'Believe on the Lord Jesus Christ and thou shalt be saved' (*Acts 16, v. 31*) was a subject dear to the heart of Charles Haddon Spurgeon. It was a great concern to him that so often this glorious simplicity was unintentionally clouded in some way or another. *Faith — what it is and what it leads to* gathers together Spurgeon's thinking on the matter and presents clearly and succinctly the exact nature of Christian faith and its consequences.

Not that Spurgeon made any boast that only he was able to get the message across, rather, as ever, he approaches his task with due humility and the prayer that his efforts would be blessed by the God who alone could 'grant the increase'. In his introduction he writes — 'So that I think I may say that, while faith is the simplest thing in all the world, yet it is one of the most difficult upon which to write; because from its very importance, our soul begins to tremble while speaking of it, and then we are not able to describe it so clearly as we would.'

In our own day we are surely in as much need as ever of clear writing on the Christian faith and it is the prayer of the publishers that this book will be blessed to all who may read it and that many will receive that most precious gift of eternal life through saving faith in Jesus Christ.

The publishers
1987

Faith

He that believeth on Him is not condemned

THE way of salvation is stated in Scripture in the very plainest terms, and yet, perhaps, there is no truth about which more errors have been uttered, than concerning the faith which saves the soul. Well has it been proved by experience, that all doctrines of Christ are mysterious — mysterious, not so much in themselves, but because they are hid to them that are lost, in whom the god of this world hath blinded their eyes. So plain is Scripture, that one would have said, "He that runs may read;" but so dim is man's eye, and so marred is his understanding, that the very simplest truth of Scripture he distorts and misrepresents. And indeed, my brethren, even those who know what faith is, personally and experimentally, do not always find it easy to give a good definition of it. They think they have hit the mark; and then, afterwards, they lament that they have failed. Straining themselves to describe some one part of faith, they find they have forgotten another, and in the excess of their earnestness to clear the poor sinner out of one mistake, they often lead him into a worse error. So that I think I may say that, while faith is the simplest thing in all the world, yet it is one of the most difficult upon which to write; because from its very importance, our soul begins to tremble while speaking of it, and then we are not able to describe it so clearly as we would.

I intend, by God's help, to put together sundry thoughts upon faith, each of which I may have spoken at different times, but which have not been collected before, and which, I have no doubt, have been misunderstood from the want of their having been put together in their proper consecutive order. I shall say a little on each of these points:

1 — *The object of faith;* or, to what it looks.

2 — *The reason of faith;* or, why doth any man believe, and whence does his faith come?

3 — *The ground of the sinner's faith;* or, on what ground he dares to believe on the Lord Jesus Christ.

4 — *The warrant of faith;* or, why it dares to trust in Christ.

5 — *The result of faith;* or, how it speeds when it comes to Christ.

6 — *The satisfactory declaration made in Scripture concerning those who have faith.*

7 — *Misapprehensions respecting faith, by reason of which Christians are often cast down.*

8 — *What this faith includes.*

9 — *What this faith excludes.*

Chapter 1

The Object of Faith; or, to what Faith looks

I AM told in the Word of God to believe — What am I to believe? I am bidden to look — to what am I to look? What is to be the object of my hope, belief, and confidence? — The reply is simple. The object of Faith to a sinner is *Christ Jesus*. How many make a mistake about this and think that they are to believe on *God the Father!* Now, belief in God is an after-result of faith in Jesus. We come to believe in the eternal love of the Father as the result of trusting the precious blood of the Son.

Many men say, "I would believe in Christ if I knew that I were elect." This is coming to the Father, and no man can come to the Father except by Christ. It is the Father's work to elect; you cannot come directly to him, therefore you cannot know your election until first you have believed on Christ the Redeemer, and then through redemption you can approach to the Father, and know your election.

Some, too, make the mistake of looking to the work of God *the Holy Spirit*. They look within to see if they have certain feelings, and if they find them, their faith is strong; but if their feelings have departed from them, then their faith is weak, so that they look to the work of the Spirit, which is not the object of a sinner's faith. Both the Father and the Spirit must be trusted, in order to complete redemption, but for the particular mercy of justification and pardon the blood of the Mediator is the only plea. *Christians* have to trust the Spirit after conversion, but the sinner's business, if he would be saved, is not with trusting the Spirit nor with looking to the Spirit, but looking to Christ Jesus, and to him alone. I know your salvation depends on the whole Trinity, but yet the first and immediate object of a sinner's justifying faith is neither God the Father, nor God the Holy Ghost, but God the Son, incarnate in human flesh, and offering atonement for sinners.

Hast thou the eye of faith? Then, soul, look thou to *Christ as God*. If thou wouldst be saved, believe him to be God over all, blessed for ever. Bow before him, and accept him as being "Very God of very God," for if thou doest not, thou hast no part in him.

When thou hast this believed, believe in him as *man*. Believe the wondrous story of his incarnation; rely upon the testimony of the evangelists, who declare that the Infinite was robed in the infant, that the Eternal was concealed within the mortal; that he who was King of heaven became a servant of servants and the Son of man. Believe and admire the mystery of his incarnation, for unless thou believe this, thou canst not be saved thereby.

Then specially, if thou wouldst be saved, let thy faith behold Christ in his *perfect righteousness*. See him keeping the law without blemish, obeying his Father without error; preserving his integrity without flaw. All this thou art to consider as being done on thy behalf. Thou couldst not keep the law; he kept it for thee. Thou couldst not obey God perfectly; lo! his obedience standeth in the stead of thy obedience — by it thou art saved.

But take care that thy faith mainly fixes itself upon Christ *as dying and as dead*. View the Lamb of God as dumb before his shearers; view him as the man of sorrows and acquainted with grief; go thou with him to Gethsemane, and behold him sweating drops of blood. Mark, thy faith has nothing to do with anything within thyself; the object of thy faith is nothing within thee, but a something without thee. Believe on him, then, who on yonder tree, with nailed hands and feet, pours out his life for sinners. There is the object of thy faith for justification; not in thyself, nor in anything which the Holy Spirit has done in thee, or anything he has promised to do for thee; but thou art to look to Christ and to Christ Jesus alone.

Then let thy faith behold Christ as *rising from the dead*. See him — he has borne the curse, and now he receives the justification. He dies to pay the debt; he rises that he may nail the handwriting of that discharged debt to the cross. See him ascending up on high, and behold him this day pleading before the Father's throne. He is there pleading for his people, offering up today his authoritative petition for all that come to God by him. And he, as God, as man, as living, as dying, as rising, and as reigning above — he, and he alone, is to be the object of thy faith for the pardon of sin.

On nothing else must thou trust; he is to be the only prop and pillar of thy confidence; and all thou addest thereunto will be a wicked anti-christ, a rebellion against the sovereignty of the Lord Jesus. But take care if your faith save you, that while you look to Christ in all these matters you view him as being *a substitute*.

This doctrine of substitution is so essential to the whole plan of salvation that I must explain it here for the thousandth time. God is just, he must punish sin; God is merciful, he wills to pardon those who believe in Jesus. How is this to be done? How can he be just and exact the penalty; merciful, and accept the sinner? He doeth it thus: he taketh the sins of his people and actually lifteth them up from off his people to Christ, so that they stand as innocent as though they had never sinned, and Christ is looked upon by God as though he had been all the sinners in the world rolled into one. The sin of his people was taken from their persons, and really and actually, not typically and metaphorically, but really and actually laid on Christ. Then God came forth with his fiery sword to meet the sinner and to punish him. He met Christ. Christ was not a sinner himself; but the sins of his people were all imputed to him. Justice, therefore, met Christ as though he had been the sinner — punished Christ for his people's sins — punished him as far as its rights could go — exacted from him the last atom of the penalty, and left not a dreg in the cup.

And now, he who can see Christ as being his

substitute, and puts his trust in him, is thereby delivered from the curse of the law. Soul, when thou seest Christ obeying the law, thy faith is to say, "He obeys that for his people." When thou seest him dying, thou art to count the purple drops, and say, "Thus he took my sins away." When thou seest him rising from the dead, thou art to say, "He rises as the head and representative of all his elect;" and when thou seest him sitting at the right hand of God, thou art to view him there as the pledge that all for whom he died shall most surely sit at the Father's right hand. Learn to look on Christ as being in God's sight as though he were the sinner. "In him was no sin." He was "*the just,*" but he suffered for the unjust. He was the righteous, but he stood in the place of the unrighteous; and all that the unrighteous ought to have endured, Christ has endured once for all, and put away their sins for ever by the sacrifice of himself.

Now, this is the great object of faith. I pray you, do not make any mistake about this, for a mistake here will be dangerous, if not fatal. View Christ, by your faith, as being in his life, and death, and sufferings, and resurrection, the substitute for all whom his Father gave him — the vicarious sacrifice for the sins of all those who will trust him with their souls. Christ, then, thus set forth, is the object of justifying faith.

Now let me further remark that there are some who may read this, no doubt, who will say — "Oh, I should believe and I should be saved if" — If what? If Christ had died? "Oh no, sir, my doubt is nothing about Christ." I thought so. Then what is the doubt? "Why, I should believe *if I felt this, or if I had done that.*" Just so; but I tell you, you could not believe in Jesus if you felt that, or if you had done that, for then you would believe in yourself, and not in Christ. That is the English of it. If you were so-and-so, or so-and-so, then you could have confidence. Confidence in what? Why, confidence in your feelings, and confidence in your doings, and that is just the clear contrary of confidence in Christ.

Faith is not to infer from something good within me that I shall be saved, but to say in the teeth, and despite of the fact, that I am guilty in the sight of God, and deserve his wrath, yet I do nevertheless believe that the blood of Jesus Christ his Son, cleanseth me from all sin; and though my present consciousness condemns me, yet my faith over-powers my consciousness, and I do believe that "he is able to save to the uttermost them that come unto God by him." To come to Christ as a saint is very easy work; to trust to a doctor to cure you when you believe you are getting better, is very easy; but to trust your physician when you feel as if the sentence of death were in your body, to bear up when the disease is rising into the very skin, and when the ulcer is gathering its venom, to believe even then in the efficacy of the medicine — that is faith.

And so, when sin gets the master of thee, when thou feelest that the law condemns thee, then, even then, as a sinner, to trust Christ, this is the most daring feat in all the world; and the faith which shook down the walls of Jericho, the faith which raised the dead, the faith which stopped the mouths of lions, was not greater than that of a poor sinner, when in the teeth of all his sins he dares to trust the blood and righteousness of Jesus Christ. Do this, soul, then thou art saved, whosoever thou mayest be. The object of faith, then, is Christ as the substitute for sinners. God in Christ, but not God apart from Christ, nor any work of the Spirit, but the work of Jesus only must be viewed by you as the foundation of your hope.

Chapter 2

The Reason of Faith; or, why doth any man believe, and whence doth his faith come?

"FAITH cometh by *hearing*." Granted, but do not all men hear, and do not many still remain unbelieving? How, then, doth any man come by his faith? To his own experience his faith comes as the result of *a sense of need*. He feels himself needing a Saviour; he finds Christ to be just such a Saviour as he wants, and therefore because he cannot help himself, he believes in Jesus. Having nothing of his own, he feels he must take Christ or else perish, and therefore he doth it because he cannot help doing it. He is fairly driven up into a corner, and there is but this one way of escape, namely, by the righteousness of another; for he feels he cannot escape by any good deeds, or sufferings of his own, and he cometh to Christ and humbleth himself, because he cannot do without Christ, and must perish unless he lay hold of him.

But to carry the question further back, where does that man get his sense of need? How is it that *he*, rather than others, feels his need of Christ! It is certain he has no more necessity for Christ than other men. How doth he come to know, then, that he is lost and ruined? How is it that he is driven by the sense of ruin to take hold on Christ the restorer? The reply is, this is *the gift of God*; this is the work of the Spirit. No man comes to Christ except the Spirit draw him, and the Spirit draws men to Christ by shutting them up under the law to a conviction that if they do not come to Christ they must perish. Then by sheer stress of weather, they tack about and run into this heavenly port. Salvation by Christ is so disagreeable to our carnal mind, so inconsistent with our love of human merit, that we never would take Christ to be our all in all, if the Spirit did not convince us that we were nothing at all, and did not so compel us to lay hold on Christ.

But, then, the question goes further back still; how is it that the Spirit of God teaches some men their need, and not other men? Why is it that some of you were driven by your sense of need to Christ, while others go on in their self-righteousness and perish? There is no answer to be given but this, "Even so, Father, for so it seemed good in thy sight." It comes to divine sovereignty at the last. The Lord hath "hidden those things from the wise and prudent, and hath revealed them unto babes." According to the way in which Christ put it — "My sheep hear my voice;" "ye believe not because ye are not of my sheep, as I said unto you." Some divines would like to read that — "Ye are not my sheep, because ye do not believe." As if believing made us the sheep of Christ; but the text puts it — "Ye believe not because ye are not of my sheep." "*All* that the Father giveth me shall come to me." If they come not, it is a clear proof that they were never given; for those who were given of old eternity to Christ, chosen of God the Father, and then redeemed by God the Son — these are led by the Spirit, through a sense of need, to come and lay hold on Christ.

No man yet ever did, or ever will believe in Christ, unless he feels his need of him. No man ever did, or will feel his need of Christ, unless the Spirit makes him feel, and the Spirit will make no man feel his need of Jesus savingly, unless it be written in that eternal book, in which God hath surely engraved the names of his chosen. So, then, I think I am not to be misunderstood on this point, that the reason of faith, or why men believe, is God's electing love working through the Spirit by a sense of need, and so bring them to Christ Jesus.

Chapter 3

The Ground of the Sinner's Faith; or, on what ground he dares to believe on the Lord Jesus Christ

MY dear friends, I have already said that no man will believe in Jesus, unless he feels his need of him. I have often said, and I repeat it again, that I do not come to Christ pleading that I *feel* my need of him; my reason for believing in Christ, is not that I *feel* my need of him, but that I *have* a need of him. The ground on which a man comes to Jesus, is not as a sensible sinner, but as a sinner, and nothing but a sinner. He will not come unless he is awakened; but when he comes, he does not say, "Lord, I come to thee because I am an awakened sinner, save me." But he says, "Lord, I am a sinner, save me." Not his awakening, but his sinnership is the method and plan upon which he dares to come.

You will, perhaps, perceive what I mean, for I cannot exactly explain myself just now, if I refer to the preaching of a great many Calvinistic divines, they say to a sinner, "Now, *if you feel* your need of Christ, *if* you have repented so much, *if* you have been harrowed by the law to such and such a degree, then you may come to Christ on the ground that you are an awakened sinner." I say that is false. No man may come to Christ on the ground of his being an awakened sinner; he must come to him *as a sinner*. When I come to Jesus, I know I cannot come unless I am awakened, but still I do not come *as* an awakened sinner. I do not stand at the foot of his cross to be washed because I have repented; I bring nothing when I come but sin. A sense of need is a good feeling, but when I stand at the foot of the cross, I do not believe in Christ because I have got good feelings, but I believe in him whether I have good feelings or not.

> Just as I am without one plea,
> But that thy blood was shed for me,
> And that thou bidst me come to thee,
> O Lamb of God I come.

Mr Roger, Mr Sheppard, Mr Flavell, and several excellent divines, in the Puritanic age, and especially Richard Baxter, used to give descriptions of what a man must feel before he may dare to come to Christ. Now, I say in the language of good Mr Fenner, another of those divines, who said he was but a babe in grace when compared with them — "I dare to say it, that all this is not Scriptural. Sinners do feel these things before they come, but they do not come on the ground of having felt it; they come on the ground of being sinners, and on no other ground whatever." The gate of mercy is opened, and over the door it is written, "This is a faithful saying and worthy of all acceptation, that Christ Jesus came into the world to save *sinners*."

Between that word "save" and the next word "sinners", there is no adjective. It does not say, "penitent sinners", "awakened sinners", "sensible sinners", "grieving sinners", or, "alarmed sinners". No, it only says "sinners", and I know this, that when I come, I come to Christ today, for I feel it is as much a necessity of my life to come to the cross of Christ today as it was to come ten years ago; when I come to him I dare not come as a conscious sinner, or an awakened sinner, but I have to come still as a sinner with nothing in my hands. I saw an aged man lately in the vestry of a chapel in Yorkshire. I had been saying something to this effect: the old man had been a Christian for years, and he said, "I never saw it put exactly so, but still I know that is just the way I come; I say, 'Lord,

> Nothing in my hands I bring,
> Simply to thy cross I cling;
> Naked, look to thee for dress;
> Helpless, come to thee for grace;
> Black —

("Black enough," said the old man.)

> I to the fountain fly,
> Wash me, Saviour, or I die."

Faith is getting right out of yourself and getting into Christ. I know that many hundreds of poor souls have been troubled because the minister has said, "if you feel your need, you may come to Christ." "But," say they, "I do not feel my need enough; I am sure I do not." Many a score letters have I received from poor troubled consciences who have said, "I would venture to believe in

Christ to save me if I had a tender conscience; if I had a soft heart; but oh, my heart is like a rock of ice which will not melt. I cannot feel as I would like to feel, and therefore I must not believe in Jesus." Oh! down with it, down with it! It is a wicked anti-Christ; it is flat Popery! It is not your soft heart that entitles you to believe. You are to believe in Christ to renew your hard heart, and come to him with nothing about you but sin.

The ground on which a sinner comes to Christ is that he is black; that he is dead, and not that he knows he is dead; that he is lost, and not that he knows he is lost. I know he will not come unless he does know it, but that is not the ground on which he comes. It is the secret reason why, but it is not the public positive ground which he understands. Here was I, year after year, afraid to come to Christ because I thought I did not feel enough; and I used to read that hymn of Cowper's about being insensible as steel —

> If aught is felt 'tis only pain
> To find I cannot feel.

When I believed in Christ, I thought I did not feel at all. *Now* when I look back I find that I had been feeling all the while most acutely and intensely, and most of all because I thought I did not feel.

Generally the people who repent the most, think they are impenitent, and people feel most their need when they think they do not feel at all, for we are no judges of our feelings, and hence the gospel invitation is not put upon the ground of anything of which we can be a judge; it is put on the ground of our being sinners, and nothing but sinners.

"Well," says one, "but it says 'Come unto me all ye that are weary and heavy-laden and I will give you rest' — then we must be weary and heavy-laden." Just so; so it is in that text, but then there is another, "Whosoever will let him come;" and that does not say anything about "weary and heavy-laden".

Besides, while the invitation is given to the weary and heavy-laden, you will perceive that the promise is not made to them *as* weary and heavy-laden, but it is made to them *as* coming to Christ. They did not know that they were weary and heavy-laden when they came; they thought they were not. They really were, but part of their weariness was that they could not be as weary as they would like to be, and part of their load was that they did not feel their load enough. They came to Christ just as they were, and he saved them, not because there was any merit in their weariness, or any efficacy in their being heavy-laden, but he saved them as sinners and nothing but sinners, and so they were washed in his blood and made clean. My dear reader, do let me put this truth home to thee. If thou wilt come to Christ, as nothing but a sinner, he will not cast thee out.

Old Tobias Crisp says in one of his sermons upon this very point, "I dare to say it, but if thou dost come to Christ, whosoever thou mayest be, if he does not receive thee, then he is not true to his word, for he says, 'Him that cometh to me I will in no wise cast out'." If thou comest, never mind qualification or preparation. He needeth no qualification of duties or of feelings either. Thou art to come just as thou art, and if thou art the biggest sinner out of hell, thou art as fit to come to Christ as if thou wert the most moral and most excellent of men. There is a bath: who is fit to be washed? A man's blackness is no reason why he should not be washed, but the clearer reason why he should be. When our City magistrates were giving relief to the poor, nobody said, "I am so poor, therefore I am not fit to have relief." Your poverty is your preparation, the black is the white here. Strange contradiction! The only thing you can bring to Christ is your sin and your wickedness. All he asks is, that you will come empty. If you have nothing of your own, you must leave all before you come. If there be anything good in you, you cannot trust Christ, you must come with nothing in your hand. Take him as all in all, and that is the only ground upon which a poor soul can be saved — as a sinner, and nothing but a sinner.

Chapter 4

The Warrant of Faith; or, why it dares to trust in Christ

IS it not imprudent for any man to trust Christ to save him, and especially when he has no good thing whatever? Is it not an arrogant presumption for any man to trust Christ? No, sirs, it is not. It is a grand and noble work of God the Holy Spirit for a man to give the lie to all his sins, and still to believe and set to his seal that God is true, and believe in the virtue of the blood of Jesus. But why does any man dare to believe in Christ? I will ask you now. "Well," saith one man, "I summoned faith to believe in Christ because I did feel there was a work of the Spirit in me." You do not believe in Christ at all. "Well," says another, "I thought that I had a right to believe in Christ, because I felt somewhat." You had not any right to believe in Christ at all on such a warranty as that.

What is a man's warrant then for believing in Christ? Here it is. Christ tells him to do it, that is his warrant. Christ's word is the warrant of the sinner for believing in Christ — not what he feels nor what he is, nor what he is not, but that Christ has told him to do it. The Gospel runs thus: "Believe on the Lord Jesus Christ and thou shalt be saved. He that believeth not shall be damned."

Faith in Christ then is a commanded duty as well as a blessed privilege, and what a mercy it is that it is a duty because there never can be any question but that a man has a right to do his duty. Now on the ground that God commands me to believe, I have a right to believe, be I who I may. The gospel is sent to every creature. Well, I belong to that tribe; I am one of the every creatures, and that gospel commands me to believe, and I do it. I cannot have done wrong in doing it, for I was commanded to do so. I cannot be wrong in obeying a command of God.

Now it is a command of God given to every creature that he should believe on Jesus Christ, whom God hath sent. This is your warrant, sinner, and a blessed warrant it is, for it is one which hell cannot gainsay, and which heaven cannot withdraw. You need not be looking within to look for the misty warrants of your experience, you need not be looking to your works, and to your feelings, to get some dull and insufficient warrants for your confidence in Christ. You may believe Christ because he tells you to do so. That is a sure ground to stand on, and one which admits of no doubt.

I will suppose that we are all starving; that the city has been besieged and shut up, and there has been a long, long famine, and we are ready to die of hunger. There comes out an invitation to us to repair at once to the palace of some great one, there to eat and drink; but we have grown foolish, and will not accept the invitation. Suppose now that some hideous madness has got hold of us, and we prefer to die, and had rather starve than come.

Suppose the king's herald should say, "Come and feast, poor hungry souls, and because I know you are unwilling to come, I add this threat, if you come not my warriors shall be upon you; they shall make you feel the sharpness of their swords." I think, my dear friends, we should say, "We bless the great man for that threatening, because now we need not say, 'I may not come,' while the fact is we may not stop away. Now I need not say I am not fit to come, for I am commanded to come, and I am threatened if I do not come; and I will even go."

That awful sentence — "He that believeth not shall be damned," was added not out of anger, but because the Lord knew our silly madness, and that we should refuse our own mercies unless he thundered at us to make us come to the feast. "Compel them to come in;" this was the Word of the Master of old, and that text is part of the carrying out of that exhortation, "Compel them to come in." Sinner, you cannot be lost by trusting Christ, but you will be lost if you do not trust him, ay, and lost for not trusting him. I put it boldly now; sinner, not only may you come, but oh! I pray you, do not defy the wrath of God by refusing to come. The gate of mercy stands wide open; why will you not come? Why will you not? Why so proud? Why will you still refuse his voice and perish in your sins? Mark, if you perish, any one of you, your blood lies not at God's door, nor Christ's door, but at your own. He can say of you, "Ye will not come unto me that ye might have life." Oh! poor trembler, if thou be willing to come, there is nothing in God's Word to keep thee from coming, but there are both threatenings to drive thee, and powers to draw thee.

Still I hear you say, "I must not trust Christ." You *may*, I say, for every creature under heaven is commanded to do it, and what you are commanded to do, you may do. "Ah! well," saith one, "still I do not feel that I may." There you are again; you say you will not do what God tells you, because of some stupid feelings of your own. You are not told to trust Christ because you feel anything, but simply because you are a sinner.

Now you know you are a sinner. "I am," says one, "and that is my sorrow." Why your sorrow? That is some sign that you do feel. "Ay," saith one, "but I do not feel enough, and that is why I sorrow. I do not feel as I should." Well, suppose you do feel, or suppose you do not, you are a sinner, and "this is a faithful saying and worthy of all acceptation that Christ Jesus came into the world to save sinners."

"Oh, but I am such an old sinner; I have been sixty years in sin." Where is it written that after sixty you cannot be saved? Sir, Christ could save you at a hundred — ay, if you were a Methuselah in guilt. "The blood of Jesus Christ his Son cleanseth us from all sin." "Whosoever will let him come." "He is able to save to the uttermost them that come unto God by him."

"Yes," says one, "but I have been a drunkard, a swearer, or lascivious, or profane." Then you are a sinner, you have not gone further than the uttermost, and he is able to save you still. "Ay," saith another, "but you do not know how my guilt has been aggravated." That only proves you to be a sinner, and that you are commanded to trust Christ and be saved. "Ay," cries yet another, "but you do not know how often I have rejected Christ." Yes, but that only makes you the more a sinner. "You do not know how hard my heart is." Just so, but that only proves you to be a sinner, and still proves you to be one whom Christ came to save.

"Oh, but sir, I have not any good thing. If I had, you know, I should have something to encourage me." The fact of your not having any good thing just proves to me that you are the man I am sent to preach to. Christ came to save that which was lost, and all you have said only proves that you are lost, and therefore he came to save you. Do trust him; do trust him.

"But if I am saved," saith one, "I shall be the biggest sinner that ever was saved." Then the greater music in heaven when you get there; the more glory to Christ, for the bigger the sinner the more honour to Christ when at last he shall be brought home. "Ay, but my sin has abounded." His grace shall much more abound. "But my sin has reached even to heaven." Yes, but his mercy reaches above the heavens. "Oh! but my guilt is as broad as the world." Yes, but his righteousness is broader than a thousand worlds. "Ay, but my sin is scarlet." Yes, but his blood is more scarlet than your sins, and can wash the scarlet out by a richer scarlet. "Ay, but I deserve to be lost, and death and hell cry for my damnation." Yes, and so they may, but the blood of Jesus Christ can cry louder than either death or hell; and it cries today, "Father, let the sinner live."

Oh! I wish I could get this thought out of my own mouth, and get it into your heads, that when God saves you, it is not because of anything in you, it is because of something in himself. God's love has no reason except in his own bowels; God's reason for pardoning a sinner is found in his own heart, and not in the sinner. And there is as much reason in you why you should be saved as why another should be saved, namely, no reason at all. There is no reason in you why he should have mercy on you, but there is no reason wanted, for the reason lies in God and in God alone.

Chapter 5

The Result of Faith; or, how it speeds when it comes to Christ

THERE is a man there who has just this momemt believed; he is not condemned. But he has been fifty years in sin, and has plunged into all manner of vice; his sins, which are many, are all forgiven him. He stands in the sight of God now as innocent as though he had never sinned. Such is the power of Jesus' blood, that "he that believeth is not condemned." Does this relate to what is to happen at the day of Judgment? I pray you look at God's Word and you will find it does not say, "He that believeth *shall* not be condemned," but he *is* not; he is not now. And if he is not now, then it follows that he never shall be; for having believed in Christ, that promise still stands, "He that believeth is not condemned." I believe today I am not condemned; in fifty years' time that promise will be just the same — "He that believeth is not condemned."

So that the moment a man puts his trust in Christ, he is freed from all condemnation — past, present, and to come; and from that day he stands in God's sight as though he were without spot or wrinkle, or any such thing. "But he sins," you say.

He does, indeed, but his sins are not laid to his charge. They were laid to the charge of Christ of old, and God can never charge the offence on two — first on Christ, and then on the sinner. "Ay, but he often falls into sin." That may be possible; though if the Spirit of God be in him he sinneth not as he was wont to do. He sins by reason of infirmity, not by reason of his love to sin, for now he hateth it.

But mark, you shall put it in your own way if you will, and I will answer, "Yes, but though he sin, yet is he no more guilty in the sight of God, for all his guilt has been taken from him, and put on Christ — positively, literally and actually lifted off from him and put upon Jesus Christ." Do you see the Jewish host? There is a scapegoat brought out; the high priest confesses the sin of the people over the scapegoat's head. The sin is all gone from the people, and laid upon the scapegoat. Away goes the scapegoat into the wilderness. Is there any sin left on the people? If there be, then the scapegoat has not carried it away. Because it cannot be *here* and *there* too. It cannot be carried away and left behind too. "No," say you, "Scripture says the scapegoat carried away the sin; there was none left on the people when the scapegoat had taken away the sin."

And so, when by faith we put our hand upon the head of Christ, does Christ take away our sin, or does he not? If he does not, then it is of no use our believing in him; but if he doth really take away our sin, then our sin cannot be on him and on us too; if it be on Christ, we are free, clear, accepted, justified, and this is the true doctrine of justification by faith. As soon as a man believeth in Christ Jesus, his sins are gone from him, and gone away for ever. They are blotted out now.

What if a man owe a hundred pounds, yet if he has got a receipt for it, he is free; it is blotted out; there is an erasure made in the book, and the debt is gone. Though the man commit sin, yet the debt having been paid before even the debt was incurred, he is no more a debtor to the law of God.

Doth not Scripture say, "That God has cast his people's sins into the depths of the sea." Now, if they are in the depths of the sea, they cannot be on his people too. Blessed be his name, in the day when he casts our sins into the depth of the sea, he views us as pure in his sight, and we stand accepted in the beloved. Then he says, "As far as the east is from the west, so far hath he removed our transgressions from us." They cannot be removed and be here still.

Then, if thou believest in Christ, thou art no more in the sight of God a sinner; thou art accepted as though thou wert perfect, as though thou hadst kept the law; for Christ has kept it, and his righteousness is thine. You have broken it, but your sin is his, and he has been punished for it. Mistake not yourselves any longer; you are no more what you were; when you believe, you stand in Christ's stead, even as Christ of old stood in your stead. The transformation is complete, the exchange is positive and eternal. They who believe in Jesus are as much accepted of God the Father as even his Eternal Son is accepted; and they that believe not, let them do what they will, they shall but go about to work out their own righteousness; but they abide under the law, and still shall they be under the curse. Now, ye that believe in Jesus, walk up and down the earth in the glory of this great truth. You are sinners in yourselves, but you are washed in the blood of Christ.

David says, "Wash me, and I shall be whiter than snow." You have seen the snow come down — how clear! how white! What could be whiter? Why, the Christian is whiter than that. You say, "He is black." I know he is as black as anyone, as black as hell; but the blood-drop falls on him, and he is as white, "whiter than snow."

The next time you see the snow-white crystals falling from heaven, look on them and say, "Ah, though I must confess within myself that I am unworthy and unclean, yet, believing in Christ, he hath given me his righteousness so completely, that I am even whiter than the snow as it descends from the treasury of God."

Oh! for faith to lay hold on this. Oh! for an overpowering faith that shall get the victory over doubts and fears, and make us enjoy the liberty wherewith Christ makes men free. Oh ye that believe in Christ, go to your beds this night, and say, "If I die in my bed I cannot be condemned." Should you wake the next morning, go into the world and say, "I am not condemned." When the devil howls at you, tell him, "Ah! you may accuse, but I am not condemned." And if sometimes your sins rise — say, "Ay, I know you, but you are all gone for ever; I am not condemned." And when your turn shall come to die shut your eyes in peace.

> Bold shall you stand in that great day,
> For who aught to your charge can lay?

Fully absolved, by grace, you shall be found at last, and all sin's tremendous curse and blame shall be taken away, not because of anything you have done. I pray you do all you can for Christ out of gratitude; but, even when you have done all, do not rest there. Rest still in the substitution and the sacrifice. Be you what Christ was in his Father's sight, and when conscience awakens, you can tell it that Christ was for you all that you ought to have been, that he has suffered all your penalty; and now neither mercy nor justice can smite you, since justice has clasped hands with mercy in a firm degree to save that man whose faith is in the cross of Christ.

Chapter 6

The Satisfactory Declaration made in Scripture concerning those who have Faith

YOU are aware that in our courts of law, a verdict of "*not guilty*" amounts to an acquittal, and the prisoner is immediately discharged. So is it in the language of the gospel; a sentence of "*not condemned*" implies the justification of the sinner. It means that the believer in Christ receives *now* a *present* justification. Faith does not produce its fruits by-and-by, but *now*. So far as justification is the result of faith, it is given to the soul in the moment when it closes with Christ, and accepts him as its all in all. Are they who stand before the throne of God justified today? So are we, as truly and as clearly justified as they who walk in white and sing his praises above. The thief upon the cross was justified the moment that he turned the eye of faith to Jesus, who was just then hanging by his side: and Paul, the aged, after years of service, was not more justified than was the thief with no service at all.

We are *today* accepted in the Beloved, *today* absolved from sin, *today* innocent in the sight of God. Oh, ravishing, soul-transporting thought!

There are some clusters of this vine which we shall not be able to gather till we go to heaven; but this is one of the first ripe clusters, and may be plucked and eaten here. This is not as the corn on the land, which we can never eat till we cross the Jordan: but this is part of the manna in the wilderness, and part, too, of our daily raiment, with which God supplies us in our journeying to and fro.

We are *now* — even *now* pardoned; even *now* are our sins put away; even *now* we stand in the sight of God as though we had never been guilty; innocent as Father Adam when he stood in integrity, ere he had eaten of the fruit of the forbidden tree; pure as though we had never received the taint of depravity in our veins. "There is, therefore, *now* no condemnation to them which are in Christ Jesus." There is not a sin in the Book of God, even *now*, against one of his people. There is nothing laid to their charge. There is neither speck, nor spot, nor wrinkle, nor any such thing remaining upon any one believer in the matter of justification in the sight of the Judge of all the earth.

But to pass on: there is not simply present, but *continual*, justification. In the moment when you and I believed, it was said of us, "He is not condemned." Many days have passed since then, many changes we have seen, but it is true of us today, "He is not condemned." The Lord alone knows how long our appointed day shall be — how long ere we shall fulfil the hireling's time, and, like a shadow, flee away. But this we know, since every word of God is assured, and the gifts of God are without repentance, though we should live another fifty years, yet would it still be written here, "He that believeth on him is not condemned." Nay, if by some mysterious dealing in providence our lives should be lengthened out to ten times the usual limit of man, and we should come to the eight or nine hundred years of Methuselah, still would it stand the same — "He that believeth on him is not condemned." "I give unto my sheep eternal life, and they shall never perish, neither shall any pluck them out of my hand." "The just shall live by faith." "He that believeth on him shall never be confounded."

All these promises go to show that the justification which Christ gives to our faith is a continual one, which will last as long as we shall live. And, remember, it will last in eternity as well as in time. We shall not in heaven wear any other dress but that which we wear here. Today the righteous stand clothed in the righteousness of Christ. They shall wear the same wedding-dress at the great wedding feast. But what if it should wear out? What if that righteousness should lose its virtue in the eternity to come? Oh, beloved! we entertain no fear about that. Heaven and earth shall pass away, but his righteousness shall never wax old. No moth shall fret it; no thief shall steal it; no weeping hand of lamentation shall rend it in twain. It is, it must be eternal, even as Christ himself, Jehovah our righteousness. Because he is our righteousness, the self-existent, the everlasting, the immutable Jehovah, of whose years there is no end, and whose strength faileth not, therefore of our righteousness there is no end; and of its perfection, and of its beauty there shall never be any termination. Scripture, I think, very clearly teaches us, that he who believeth in Christ has received for ever a continual justification.

Again, think for a moment: this justification is *complete*. "He that believeth on him is not condemned;" that is to say not in any measure or in any degree. I know some think it is possible for us to be in such a state as to be half-condemned and half-accepted. So far as we are sinners, so far condemned; and so far as we are righteous, so far accepted. Oh, beloved, there is nothing like that in Scripture. It is altogether apart from the doctrine of the gospel. If it be of works, it is no more of grace; and if it be of grace, it is no more of works. Works and grace cannot mix and mingle any more than fire and water; it is either one or the other, it cannot be both; the two can never be allied. There can be no admixture of the two, no dilution of one with the other.

He that believeth is free from all iniquity, from all guilt, from all blame; and though the devil bring an accusation, yet it is a false one, for we are free even from accusation, since it is boldly challenged, "Who shall lay anything to the charge of God's elect?" It does not say "Who shall prove it?" but "Who shall lay it to their charge?" They are so completely freed from condemnation, that not the shadow of a spot upon their soul is found; not even the slightest passing by of iniquity to cast its black shadow on them. They stand before God not only as half-innocent, but as perfectly so; not only as half-washed, but as whiter than snow. Their sins are not simply erased, they are blotted out; not simply put out of sight, but cast into the depths of the sea; not merely gone, and gone as far as the east is from the west, but gone for ever, once for all.

You know, beloved, that the Jew in his ceremonial purification, never had his conscience free from sin. After one sacrifice he needed still another, for these offerings could never make the comers thereunto perfect. The next day's sins needed a new lamb, and the next year's iniquity needed a new victim for an atonement. "But this man, after he had offered one sacrifice for sins for ever, sat down at the right hand of God." No more burnt-offerings are needed, no more washing, no more blood, no more atonement, no more sacrifice. "It is finished!" hear the dying Saviour cry. Your sins have sustained their death-blow, the robe of your righteousness has received its last thread; it is done, complete, perfect. It needs no addition; it can never suffer any diminution.

Oh, Christian, do lay hold of this precious thought; I may not be able to state it except in weak terms, but let not my weakness prevent your apprehending its glory and its preciousness. It is enough to make a man leap, though his legs were loaded with irons, and to make him sing, though his mouth were gagged, to think that we are perfectly accepted in Christ, that our justification is not partial; it does not go to a limited extent, but goes the whole way. Our unrighteousness is covered; from condemnation we are entirely and irrevocably free.

Once more. The non-condemnation is *effectual*.

The royal privilege of justification shall never miscarry. It shall be brought home to every believer. In the reign of King George the Third, the son of a member of my church lay under sentence of death for forgery. My predecessor, Dr. Rippon, after incredible exertions, obtained a promise that his sentence should be remitted. By a singular occurrence the present senior deacon — then a young man — learned from the governor of the gaol that the reprieve had not been received; and the unhappy prisoner would have been executed the next morning, had not Dr. Rippon gone post-haste to Windsor, obtained an interview with the king in his bed-chamber, and received from the monarch's own hand a copy of that reprieve which had been negligently put aside by a thoughtless officer. "I charge you, Doctor," said his majesty, "to make good speed." "Trust me, Sire, for that," responded the Doctor, and he returned to London in time, and only just in time, for the prisoner was being marched with many others on to the scaffold.

Ay, that pardon might have been given, and yet the man might have been executed if it had not been effectually carried out. But blessed be God our non-condemnation is an effectual thing. It is not a matter of letter, it is a matter of fact. Ah, poor souls, you know that condemnation is a matter of fact. When you and I suffered in our souls, and were brought under the heavy hand of the law, we felt that its curses were no mock thunders like the wrath of the Vatican, but they were real; we felt that the anger of God was indeed a thing to tremble at; a real substantial fact.

Now, just as real as the condemnation which Justice brings, just so real is the justification which mercy bestows. You are not only nominally guiltless, but you are really so, if you believe in Christ; you are not only nominally put into the place of the innocent, but you are really put there the moment you believe in Jesus. Not only is it said that your sins are gone, but they are gone. Not only does God look on you as though you were accepted; you are accepted. It is a matter of fact to you, as much a matter of fact as that you sinned. You do not doubt that you have sinned, you cannot doubt that; do not doubt then that when you believe your sins are put away. For as certain as ever the black spot fell on you when you sinned, so certainly and so surely was it all washed out when you were bathed in that fountain filled with blood, which was drawn from Emanuel's veins.

Come, my soul, think thou of this. Thou art actually and effectually cleared from guilt. Thou art led out of thy prison. Thou art no more in fetters as a bond-slave. Thou art delivered now from the bondage of the law. Thou art freed from sin and thou canst walk at large as a free man. Thy Saviour's blood has procured thy full discharge. Come, my soul, — thou hast a right now to come to thy Father's feet. No flames of vengeance are there to scare thee now; no fiery sword; justice cannot smite the innocent. Come, my soul, thy disabilities are taken away. Thou wast unable once to see thy Father's face; thou canst see it now. Thou couldst not speak with him, nor he with thee; but now thou hast access with boldness to this grace wherein we stand. Once there was a fear of hell upon thee; there is no hell for thee now. How can there be punishment for the guiltless? He that believeth is guiltless, is not condemned, and cannot be punished. No frowns of an avenging God now. If God be viewed as a Judge, how should he frown upon the guiltless? How should the Judge frown upon the absolved one?

More than all the privileges thou mightest have enjoyed if thou hadst never sinned, are thine now that thou art justified. All the blessings which thou couldst have had if thou hadst kept the law and more, are thine today, because Christ has kept it for thee. All the love and the acceptance which a perfectly obedient being could have obtained of God, belong to thee, because Christ was perfectly obedient on thy behalf, and this imputed all his merits to thy account that thou mightest be exceedingly rich through him who for thy sake became exceeding poor.

Oh that the Holy Spirit would but enlarge our hearts, that we might suck sweetness out of these thoughts! There is no condemnation. Moreover, there never shall be any condemnation. The forgiveness is not partial, but perfect; it is so effectual that it delivers us from all the penalties of the Law, gives to us all the privileges of obedience, and puts us actually high above where we should have been had we never sinned. It fixes our standing more secure than it was before we fell. We are not now where Adam was, for Adam might fall and perish. We are, rather, where Adam would have been if we could suppose God had put him into the garden for seven years, and said, "If you are obedient for seven years, your time of probation shall be over, and I will reward you."

The children of God in one sense may be said to be in a state of probation; in another sense there is no probation. There is no probation as to whether the child of God shall be saved. He is saved already; his sins are washed away; his righteousness is complete: and if that righteousness could endure a million of years' probation, it would never be defiled. In fact it always stands the same in the sight of God and must do so for ever and ever.

Chapter 7

Misapprehensions respecting it, by reasons of which Christians are often cast down

WHAT simpletons we are! Whatever our natural age, how childish we are in spiritual things! What great simpletons we are when we first believe in Christ! We think that our being pardoned involves a great many things which we afterwards find have nothing whatever to do with our pardon. For instance, we think we shall never sin again; we fancy that the battle is all fought; that we have got into a fair field, with no more war to wage; that in fact we have got the victory, and have only just to stand up and wave the palm branch; that all is over; that God has only got to call us up to himself, and we shall enter into heaven without having to fight any enemies upon earth.

Now, all these are obvious mistakes. Observe that although it is asserted "He that believeth is not condemned;" yet it is not said that he that believeth shall not have his faith exercised. Your faith will be exercised. An untried faith will be no faith at all. God never gave men faith without intending to try it. Faith is received for the very purpose of endurance. Just as our Rifle Corps friends put up the target with the intention of shooting at it: so does God give faith with the intention of letting trials and troubles, and sin and Satan aim all their darts at it. When thou hast faith in Christ it is a great privilege; but recollect that it involves a great trial. You asked for great faith the other night; did you consider that you asked for great troubles too? You cannot have great faith to lay up and rust.

Mr Greatheart, in John Bunyan's Pilgrim, was a very strong man, but then what strong work he had to do. He had to go with all those women and children many scores of times up to the celestial city and back again; he had to fight all the giants, and drive back all the lions; to slay the giant Slaygood, and knock down the Castle of Despair. If you have a great measure of faith, you will have need to use it all. You will never have a single scrap to spare, you will be like the virgins in our Lord's parable, even though you be a wise virgin, you will have to say to others who might borrow of you, "Not so, lest there be not enough for us and for you."

But when your faith is exercised with trials, do not think you are brought into judgment for your sins. Oh no, believer; there is plenty of exercise, but that is not condemnation; there are many trials, but still we are justified; we may often be buffeted, but we are never accursed; we may ofttimes be cast down, but the sword of the Lord never can and never will smite us to the heart.

Yea, more; not only may our faith be exercised, but our faith may come to a very low ebb, and still we may not be condemned. When thy faith gets so small that thou canst not see it, even then still thou art not condemned. If thou hast ever believed in Jesus, thy faith may be like the sea when it goes out a very long way from the shore, and leaves a vast track of mud, and some might say the sea was gone or dried up. But you are not condemned when your faith is most dried up. Ay! and I dare to say it, when your faith is at the flood-tide, you are not more accepted then than when your faith is at the lowest ebb; for your acceptance does not depend upon the quantity of your faith, it only depends upon its reality.

If you are really resting in Christ, though your faith may be but as a spark, and a thousand devils may try to quench that one spark, yet you are not condemned — you shall stand accepted in Christ. Though your comforts will necessarily decay as your faith declines, yet your acceptance does not decay. Though faith does rise and fall like the thermometer, though faith is like the mercury in the bulb, all weathers change it, yet God's love is not affected by the weather of earth, or the changes of time. Until the perfect righteousness of Christ can be a mutable thing — a football to be kicked about by the feet of fiends — your acceptance with God can never change. You are, you must be, perfectly accepted in the Beloved.

There is another thing which often tries the child of God. He at times loses the light of his Father's countenance. Now, remember, it is not said, "He that believeth shall not lose the light of God's countenance;" he may do so, but he shall not be condemned for all that. You may walk, not only for days but for months, in such a state that you have little fellowship with Christ, very little communion with God of a joyous sort; the promises may seem broken to you, the Bible may afford to you but little comfort; and when you turn your eye to heaven, you may only have to feel the more the smarting that is caused by your Father's rod; you may have vexed and grieved his Spirit, and he may have turned away his face from you; but you are not condemned for all that. Mark the testimony, "He that believeth is not condemned." Even when your Father smites you and leaves a wale at every stroke, and brings the blood at every blow, there is not a particle of condemnation in any one stroke. Not in his anger, but in his dear covenant love he smites you. There is as unmixed and unalloyed affection in every lovestroke of chastisement from your Father's hand as there is in the kisses of Jesus Christ's lips. Oh, believe this; it will tend to lift up thy heart, it will cheer thee when neither sun nor moon appear. It will honour thy God, it will show thee where thy acceptance really lies. When his face is turned away, believe him still, and say, "He abideth faithful though he hide his face from me."

I will go a little further still. The child of God may be so assaulted by Satan that he may be well nigh given up to despair, and yet he is not condemned. The devils may beat the great hell-drum in his ear, till he thinks himself to be on the very brink of perdition. He may read the Bible, and think that every threatening is against him, and that every promise shuts its mouth and will not cheer him: and he may at last despond, and despond, and despond, till he is ready to break the harp that has so long been hanging on the willow. He may say, "The Lord hath forsaken me quite, my God will be gracious no more;" but it is not true. Yea, he may be ready to swear a thousand times that God's mercy is clean gone for ever, and that his faithfulness will fail for evermore; but it is not true, it is not true. A thousand liars swearing to a falsehood could not make it true, and our doubts and fears are all of them liars. And if there were ten thousand of them, and they all professed the same, it is a falsehood that God ever did forsake his people, or that he ever cast from him an innocent man; and you are innocent, remember, when you believe in Jesus.

"But," say you, "I am full of sin." "Ay," say I, "but that sin has been laid on Christ." "Oh," say you, "but I sin daily." "Ay," say I, "but that sin was laid on him before you committed it, years ago. It is not yours; Christ has taken it away once for all. You are a righteous man by faith, and God will not forsake the righteous, nor will he cast away the innocent." I say, then, the child of God may have his faith at a low ebb; he may lose the light of his Father's countenance, and he may even get into thorough despair; but yet all these cannot disprove God's word, "He that believeth is not condemned."

"But what," say you, "if the child of God should sin?" It is a deep and tender subject, yet must we touch it and be bold here. I would not mince God's truth, lest any should make a bad use of it. I know there are some, not the people of God, who will say, "Let us sin, that grace may abound." Their condemnation is just. I cannot help the perversion of truth. There be always men who will take the best of food as though it were poison, and make the best of truth into a lie, and so be damning their own souls.

You ask, "What if a child of God should fall into sin?" I answer, the child of God does fall into sin; every day he mourns and groans because when he would do good, evil is present with him. But though he falls into sins, he is not condemned for all — not by one of them, or by all of them put together, because his acceptance does not depend upon himself, but upon the perfect righteousness of Christ; and that perfect righteousness is not invalidated by any sins of his. He is perfect in Christ; and until Christ is imperfect, the imperfections of the creature do not mar the justification of the believer in the sight of God.

But oh! if he fall into some glaring sin, — O God, keep us from it! — if he fall into some glaring sin, he shall go with broken bones, but he shall reach heaven for all that. Though, in order to try him and let him see his vileness, he be suffered to go far astray, yet he that bought him will not lose him; he that chose him will not cast him away; he will say unto him, "I, even I, am he that blotteth out thy transgressions for my own sake, and will not remember thy sins." David may go never so far away, but David is not lost. He comes back and he cries, "Have mercy upon me, O God!" And so shall it be with every believing soul — Christ shall bring him back. Though he slip, he shall be kept, and all the chosen seed shall meet around the throne.

If it were not for this last truth — though some may stick at it — what would become of some of God's people? They would be given up to despair. If, dear reader, you are a backslider, I pray you make not a bad use of what I have said. Let me say to you, Poor backslider! thy Father's bowels yearn over thee; he has not erased thy name out of the registry. Come back, come back now to him and say, "Receive me graciously, and love me freely;" and he will say, "I will put you among the children." He will pass by your backsliding and will heal your iniquities; and you shall yet stand once more in his favour, and know yourself to be still accepted in the Redeemer's righteousness and saved by his blood. God does not mean that his child shall not be tried, or that he shall not even sometimes fall under the trial; but he does mean this, once for all: he that believeth on Christ is not condemned. At no time, by no means, is he under the sentence of condemnation, but is evermore justified in the sight of God.

Chapter 8

What this Faith Includes

IF we are not condemned, then at no time does God ever look upon his children, when they believe in Christ, as being guilty. Are you surprised that I should put it so? I put it so again: from the moment when you believe in Christ, God ceases to look upon you as being guilty; for he never looks upon you apart from Christ. You often look upon yourself as guilty, and you fall upon your knees as you should do, and you weep and lament; but even then, while you are weeping over inbred and actual sin, he is still saying out of heaven, "So far as your justification is concerned, thou art all fair and lovely." You are black as the tents of Kedar — that is yourself by nature; you are fair as the curtains of Solomon — that is yourself in Christ. You are black — that is yourself in Adam: but comely, that is yourself in the second Adam.

Oh, think of that! — that you are always in God's sight comely, always in God's sight lovely, always in God's sight as though you were perfect. For ye are complete in Christ Jesus, and perfect in Christ Jesus, as the apostle puts it in another place. Always do you stand completely washed and fully clothed in Christ. Remember this; for it is certainly included in the words, "he that believeth on him is not condemned."

Another great thought is this, you are never liable as a believer to punishment for your sins. You will be chastised on account of them, as a father chastises his child; that is a part of the Gospel dispensation; but you will not be smitten for your sins as the lawgiver smites the criminal. Your Father may often punish you as he punisheth the wicked. But never for the same reason.

The ungodly stand on the ground of their own demerits; their sufferings are awarded as their due deserts. But your sorrows do not come to you as a matter of desert; they come to you as a matter of love. God knows that in one sense your sorrows are such a privilege that you may account of them as a boon you do not deserve. I have often thought of that when I have had a sore trouble. I know some people say, "You deserved the trouble." Yes, my dear brethren, but there is not enough merit in all the Christians put together, to deserve such a good thing as the loving rebuke of our heavenly Father.

Perhaps you cannot see that; you cannot think that a trouble can come to you as a real blessing in the covenant. But I know that the rod of the covenant is as much the gift of grace as the blood of the covenant. It is not a matter of desert or merit; it is given to us because we need it. But question whether we were ever so good as to deserve it. We were never able to get up to so high a standard as to deserve so rich, so gracious a providence as this covenant blessing — the rod of our chastening God. Never at any time in your life has a law-stroke fallen upon you. Since you believed in Christ you are out of the law's jurisdiction.

The law of England cannot touch a Frenchman while he lives under the protection of his own Emperor. You are not under the law, but you are under grace. The law of Sinai cannot touch you, for you are out of its jurisdiction. You are not in Sinai or in Arabia. You are not the son of Hagar, or the son of a handmaid, you are the son of Sarah, and are come to Jerusalem and are free. You are out of Arabia, and are come to God's own happy land. You are not under Hagar, but under Sarah; under God's covenant of grace. You are a child of promise, and you shall have God's own inheritance.

Believe this, that never shall a law-stroke fall on you; never shall God's anger in a judicial sense drop on you. He may give you a chastising stroke, not as the result of sin, but rather as the result of his own rich grace, that would get the sin out of you, that you may be perfected in sanctification, even as you are now perfect and complete before him in the blood and righteousness of Jesus Christ.

Chapter 9

What this Faith Excludes

WHAT does it exclude? Well, I am sure it excludes boasting. "He that believeth is not condemned." Ah! if it said, "He that *worketh* is not condemned," then you and I might boast in any quantity. But when it says, "*He that believeth*" — why, there is no room for us to say half a word for old self. No, Lord, if I am not condemned, it is thy free grace, for I have deserved to be condemned a thousand times since I sat down to write this. When I am on my knees, and I am not condemned, I am sure it must be sovereign grace, for even when I am praying I deserved to be condemned. Even when we are repenting we are sinning, and adding to our sins while we are repenting of them. Every act we do as the result of the flesh, is to sin again, and our best performances are so stained with sin that it is hard to know whether they are good works or bad works. So far as they are our own, they are bad; and so far as they are the works of the Spirit, they are good. But, then, the goodness is not ours, it is the Spirit's, and only the evil remains to us. Ah, then, we cannot boast! Begone, pride! begone!

The Christian must be a humble man. If he lift up his head to say something, then he is nothing indeed. He does not know where he is, or where he stands, when he once begins to boast, as though his own right hand had gotten him the victory. Leave off boasting, Christian; live humbly before thy God, and never let a word of self-congratulation escape thy lips. Sacrifice self, and let thy song be before the throne, "Not unto us, not unto us, but unto thy name be glory for ever."

What next does it exclude? Methinks it ought to exclude — now I am about to smite myself — it ought to exclude doubts and fears. "He that believeth is not condemned." How dare you and I draw such long faces, and go about as we do sometimes as though we had a world of cares upon our backs? What would I have given ten or eleven years ago if I could have known that text was sure to me, that I was not condemned. Why, I thought if I could feel I was once forgiven, and had to live on bread and water, and to be locked up in a dungeon, and every day be flogged with a cat-o'-nine tails, I would gladly have accepted it, if I could have once felt my sins forgiven.

Now you are a forgiven man, and yet you are cast down! Oh! shame on you. No condemnation! and yet miserable? Fie, Christian! Get thee up and wipe the tears from your eyes. Oh! if there be a person lying in gaol now, to be executed next week, if you could go to him and say, "You are pardoned," would he not spring up with delight from his seat; and although he might have lost his goods, and though it would be possible for him, after pardon, to have to suffer many things, yet, so long as life was spared, what would all this be to him? He would feel that it was less than nothing.

Now, Christian, you are pardoned, your sins are all forgiven. Christ has said to you, "Thy sins, which are many, are all forgiven thee" — and art thou yet miserable? Well, if we must be so sometimes, let us make it as short as we can. If we must be sometimes cast down, let us ask the Lord to lift us up again. I am afraid some of us get into bad habits, and come to make it a matter of practice to be downcast. Mind, Christian, mind it will grow upon you — that peevish spirit — if you do not resist that sinfulness at first, it will get worse with you. If you do not come to God to turn these doubts and fears out of you, they will soon swarm upon you like flies in Egypt. When you are able to kill the first great doubt, you will perhaps kill a hundred, for one great doubt will breed a thousand, and to kill the mother is to kill the whole brood.

Therefore, look with all thy eyes against the first doubt, lest thou shouldest become confirmed in thy despondency, and grow into sad despair. "He that believeth on him is not condemned." If this excludes boasting, it ought to exclude doubts too.

Once more. This excludes sinning any more. My Lord, have I sinned against thee so many times, and yet hast thou freely forgiven me all? What stronger motive could I have for keeping me from sinning again? Ah, there are some who are saying this is licentious doctrine. A thousand devils rolled into one, must the man be who can find any licentiousness here. What! go and sin because I am forgiven? Go and live in iniquity because Jesus Christ took my guilt and suffered in my room and stead? Human nature is bad enough, but methinks this is the very worst state of human nature, when it tries to draw an argument for sin from the free grace of God.

Bad as I am, I do feel this, that it is hard to sin against a pardoning God. It is far harder to sin against the blood of Christ, and against a sense of pardon, than it is against the terrors of the law and the fears of hell itself. I know that when my soul is most alarmed by a dread of the wrath of God, I can sin with comfort compared with what I could when I have a sense of his love shed abroad in my heart. What more monstrous! to read your title clear, and sin? Oh, vile reprobate! you are on the borders of the deepest hell. But I am sure, if you are a child of God, you will say when you have read your title clear, and feel yourself justified in Christ Jesus.

> Now, for the love I bear his name,
> What was my gain, I count my loss;
> My former pride I call my shame,
> And nail my glory to his cross.

Yes, and I must, and will esteem all things but loss for Jesus' sake. O may my soul be found in him, perfect in his righteousness! This will make you live near to him; this will make you like unto him. Do not think that this doctrine, by dwelling on it, will make you think lightly of sin. It will make you think of it as a hard and stern executioner to put Christ to death; as an awful load that could never be lifted from you except by the eternal arm of God; and then you will come to hate it with all your soul, because it is rebellion against a loving and gracious God, and you shall, by this means, far better than by any Arminian doubts or any legal quibbles, be led to walk in the footsteps of your Lord Jesus, and to follow the Lamb whithersoever he goeth.

I think this little work, though I have written it for the children of God, is meant for sinners too. Sinner, I would that thou didst say so. If you know this, that *he that believeth is not condemned*, then, sinner if thou believest thou wilt not be condemned; and may all that I have said help you to this belief in thy soul.

Oh, but sayest thou, "May I trust Christ?" As I said, it is not a question of whether you may or may not, you are commanded. The Scripture commands the gospel to be preached to every creature, and the gospel is, "Believe in the Lord Jesus Christ and thou shalt be saved." I know you will be too proud to do it, unless God by his grace should humble you. But if ye feel that you are nothing and have nothing of your own, I think you will be right glad to take Christ to be your all-in-all. If you can say with poor Jack the Huckster, —

> I'm a poor sinner and nothing at all,

You may go on and say with him,

> But Jesus Christ is my all in all.

God grant that it may be so, for his name's sake. Amen.

Also published by
Christian Focus Publications

Around the Wicket Gate

Charles Haddon Spurgeon

Around the Wicket Gate was written to those who had some knowledge of the Gospel message but as yet were outside of Christ. In Bunyan's words from *Pilgrim's Progress* they were around the wicket gate but had not entered. Out of zeal for God's glory and love to his readers Spurgeon makes it clear that to be 'almost a Christian' is a most dangerous state. Here he presents in his own compelling manner the full and free salvation of God through trust in Jesus Christ alone.